When Cyanide Tastes Sweet

J C Wood

BookLeaf Publishing

Presentation by *BookLeaf Publishing*

Web: www.bookleafpub.com

E-mail: info@bookleafpub.com

ISBN: 9789395890878

First edition 2022

PREFACE

I was 14 when I started writing poetry. At that point I had no diagnoses, no doctors, no medications. I was, however, most definitely not well. Writing poetry was the way I coped with my illness, when I had nothing else to fall back on, and no understanding of what was happening.

If you feel the way I felt, find something to hold on to. A friend, a pet, a hobby. Writing, maybe. There is a way through.

It's Just Medicine

There's a lavender filter draped over my corneas.
More blue than pink, monkswood and dust.

My history is patterned and pulsating in the
leaves of the trees, green-drained and echoic; I
can't get away even if I close my eyes. At least
the memories are soft and silent, flickering like
old film.
Nothing hurts in this liminal-blue space.

Under the Hospital Lights

I am a girl. I am a bruise. Coagulated and cold
and hidden-sticky.... no, wait, hot and seeping,
blood and tissue and emotion raw
sensitive/numb, do you understand me? I am a
contradiction, feel nothing and all too much.
Like autopsy dead flesh I'm not right on the
inside; anaesthetised when you dissect my
heart/desires/amygdala/emotions. You won't hurt
me: I have been here before, dissociated for
want of your attention.
Anguish when you turn away.

Maybe I am blooming. Adaptation in response
to trauma, deep and purple and sickly yellow. I
feel/don't feel. Maybe it's pathology but maybe it
will save me. Do you understand me? I am a
bruise. I am a girl.

Morning

To me, morning is something new: something
tentative. A realm yet unexplored.
After a decade of midday awakenings and
midnight wanderings, the frostcold in my fingers
and dappled light on the tile are just a shadow of
a memory. Something to relearn like an old
friend.

I don't know if change means growth.
I don't know if six months of silent daybreak
anaesthetises a lifetime of hollow night.

I am alone in both.
But the night held monsters, and dawn feels
kind.

Nil By Mouth

There's a drip in my arm and a tube up my nose
and I want them out.
I am vein-drowned, throat acrid/arid with
ulcerating ooze and fear.

We swim untethered in a hospital bed
archipelago: across the curtained water, the
clipboard-men blur into one faceless white coat.
They keep their distance (madness is catching),
judgement/pity/scorn/confusion shining in their
inkwells. They don't hear me beg for water. My
voice is just another machine readout to place in
the file.

Night becomes day becomes night. Dark doesn't
exist here. Neither does quiet. A carousel of
medications and blood tests and drip drip drip,
the Ward a monster's maw, taking those who
won't heal and eating them alive.

Silence

There's something hiding in the silence of the pre-dawn. An unknowable frequency, cicada drone or overheating machinery. It's a physical pressure, sharp and gluttonous and unyielding. What do you do when the silence is so loud?

Tuesday

Morning mum, time to wake up. Don't worry, I've got it. Watch the coffee, it's hot. What was that? It's Tuesday today. No, I don't have to be at school for another hour. Do you need a hand? Careful of the door frame. If you just wait a minute, I'll get the porridge off the stove and then I'll help you with the shower. Is that temperature okay? It's Tuesday today. It's fine mum, I don't mind helping. I picked out some clothes for you, it's going to be warm today. Do you want to have a bit of a rest here while I finish my homework? Don't worry, I'll stay with you, I can sit on the end of the bed. Mmm, what was that? Oh it's just math, we're doing fractions this week. Yeah, I like it. They're letting me do some middle-school math if I finish early. Do you want me to get your planner, so we can do some work at the same time? Here we go. Yeah, it's Tuesday today. Looks like you have an appointment at 3, do you want me to set an alarm for you? All done. I've put it on a post-it on your mirror as well. If you give me a second I'll get you your meds, it's almost 8. No, I didn't finish my homework but that's okay, I'll do it in the car. Don't worry, honestly. Here, take

these ones first. I know it hurts. I'll get you a hot
water bottle, will you be okay here for a minute?
Hey mum, I'm back. What, this hot water bottle?
I know, I'm like a mind reader hey? Here, sit up
a little so I can put it under your neck. I've got
to go to school mum, but I'll be back before you
think. It's Tuesday today. I love you.

Things I Have Thought Today

coffee.meds.nicotine / beatbeatbeat too fast, my tachycardia burns rampaging guilt when your chest is hollow and still / breathe in, breathe out / i need to do laundry / i need to do study / i need i need i need / focus on the smoke patterns in sunlight shafts / like mercury lustre in test tubes / stop chewing on your lips / breathe in, breathe out / dying whales create whole new ecosystems at the bottoms of oceans / when i die, will life blossom around me? / or will I spread rot like a carcass trapped in a crevice? / one valium, no, two / why haven't i heard back from you? / beatbeatbeat, you're probably fine / I'm sure everything is fine / breathe in, breathe out

Shards

Desolate or distracted -
both are dangerous;
blank stare and twitching feet,
one step closer to oblivion.

I'm a girl made of
    unlit fuses
push my buttons and
watch me explode.

Suicidal isn't the right term.
I'm volatile, fragile.
Do I scare you? When I
break be careful not to
step on the shards.

Call me crazy, I'm a hot mess
and you might never know
if I'm going to laugh or scream.

Broken

Sometimes I want to put my hand
through a pane of glass just to see
how it feels. What it looks like.
What it sounds like. I imagine it
in slow motion, diamond splinters
glittering and marred
with scarlet. Something beautiful,
tainted and shattered.
Broken.

Bastard Bleeding Bleeding Heart

I loved you, once.
Silk and water, freckles and chrome.

I think I was meant to live
a different life. It pulls at me, a
channel branching from a stream,
a memory/melody floating just out of reach.
I don't know where you live, now.
I don't know who you are.
But there's a place in the cloudbank,
where we are trapped together in a single
moment.
One of the nice ones, one of the ones where
I was bright and sparkling and you smelled
like Lynx and sun-warmed dust.
Perhaps I could live in that moment forever.
No future, no past.
No heartbreak, no hospitals, no memory.
Silk and water, freckles and chrome.

Forget Her

She wants you to forget her, like the discoloured pattern on your old carpet. She'll fall under your feet, shrink step by step, becoming cracks in the pavement.
She wants to melt away with the rain, slide down gutters and driveways, become just one drop in that frenzied rush to the sea. She wants to be the condensation on your windowpanes, watching from the outside in.
She wants to dance with her eyes closed to the music, mellow movement in a dark room.

A whisper in the curtains, she is nothing and no one. She wants you to forget her.

Insanity

Surround yourself with insanity and it becomes
you.
Or you become it - or you become each other,
twined like embracing lovers, so close you can
no longer tell which one of you is sane.

Institutionalised, you can make yourself believe
this you are safe,
that the madness is home.

Quiescence

We spend the entirety of our lives waiting to die.
Not trying, but waiting, pretending every
rotation
of the Earth around the sun has some tangible
meaning.
We are solitary fruit, rotting.

ADHD Musings

My thoughts are trains in a station:
the rushing express, the scheduled route
stopping to unload and re-form,
the out-of-service carriage that has been
hunched in the dim lighting for as long as
anyone can remember.

Trains come and go, overlapping, backlogging,
horns and metal.
Platform after platform after platform.
A steam engine fills the air with smog.
Conductors yell.
The schedules are wrong.
There are too many people.
There are too many people.

Someone jumps in front of a train.

Choked and overloaded, smoke and dust and
people and blood and bones.
Like a technical malfunction: frozen trains,
frozen thoughts, system glitch.
I blink to try and reset them. Sometimes it helps.
Sometimes I am left

with a gridlocked mind and thoughts
evaporating bone-dry on my tongue.

Medication is grease in the wheels,
synchronicity. No more than four trains in the
station at once, they wait patiently until they're
no longer needed, fading away into the night.

Want

Want is a pit, a yawning endlessness;
sinkholes in the desert, shadows in the night.
I was born without a lid for the box it dwells in,
a genetic flaw in control.
Want consumes me.
It feels like daybreak and knives: my heart is
iron and Want forms a magnet and I can't I can't
I can't resist.
So I love and run and buy and steal and gorge
and starve and drink and dance.
I am weak, and I am wanting.

Ghosts

There's a ghost in the corner of my room.
Skin dripping from bones, ash-faded in the dusk.
It's a memory given form, a nightmare blend of
truth and presumption.

We all have ghosts we choose not to see.
The earth is congested with them, cramped and
clogged like gutters overflowing in the rain. We
are a minority, beetles amongst the Gods of
memory and fear.
Choose truth. Choose to face your ghosts.
The Earth is haunted enough.

Forgotten

Love is foreign to me, shrouded in
the damp translucent fog of memory.
I know I have had it, been encompassed
by it, grieved it. I remember love.
But my memories are ink on paper,
logistical. I can't feel
the goodbad ache, the evolutionary draw,
the purity of emotion: snowmelt in burning sun.
Sometimes, I wonder if I just ran
out, my allotment used up on
teenage boys who
didn't want my kind of love.

Poetry is...

Poetry is a frangipani tree, leafless and bare, its green wick treasured and secret. It's nicotine in bottles, syrup darkened from the sun. Poetry is a girl tired from therapy, the feeling of ghost fingers riffling through her brain fading like a memory. It's rain and book-scent and dinners delivered in cardboard boxes on the doorstep, mindless tv and mindful breathing. Poetry is death's last clean shirt, soft and travel-worn and waiting.